REDBACK publishing

NATURAL DISASTERS

FLOODS IN AUSTRALIA

BY JOHN LESLEY

First Published 2026 by
Redback Publishing
Suite 6, 13a Narabang Way,
Belrose NSW 2085
Australia

www.redbackpublishing.com
orders@redbackpublishing.com

ISBN 978-1-761401-92-3

Author: John Lesley
Editor: Caroline Thomas
Designer: Redback Publishing

Acknowledgements
Abbreviations: l—left, r—right, b—bottom, t—top, c—centre, m—middle
We would like to thank the following for permission to reproduce photographs: (Images © shutterstock) p7tl Alex Cimbal, p12tr Jonathan Mace, p14c Adam Marshal, p15tl Adam Marshal, p15br Markus Gebauer, p18-19 EA Given, p19tl Maythee Voran, p19br English Wikipedia user Billbeee, CC BY-SA 3.0 (http://creativecommons.org/licenses/by-sa/3.0/), via Wikimedia Commons, p21c Alan Dunn, p22tl Silken Photography, p23tl State Library of New South Wales collection, No restrictions, via Wikimedia Commons, Kgbo, p23tr CC BY-SA 4.0 (https://creativecommons.org/licenses/by-sa/4.0), via Wikimedia Commons, p24tl The National Oceanic and Atmospheric Administration, NCDC, Public domain, via Wikimedia Commons, p24tr Markus Gebauer, p25tl Alex Cimbal, p26bl crbellette, p30bc Agriculture And Stock Department, Publicity Branch, Public domain, via Wikimedia Commons

A catalogue record for this book is available from the National Library of Australia

CONTENTS

WHAT IS A FLOOD?

A flood occurs when water overflows onto normally dry areas. These areas can be bushland, deserts, backyards, cities or inside a house. When a washing machine overflows inside, we say the laundry is flooded, although this is a much less disastrous event than a flood that covers a whole neighbourhood.

Floods become natural disasters when they are so severe that they cause environmental damage, destroy crops and stock, damage buildings, roads and bridges, and take lives.

LA NIÑA

La Niña means 'the girl' in Spanish. It is a weather pattern that in the past brought higher than average rainfall every three to five years. Known as La Niña Southern Oscillation, it has the opposite effect to El Niño Southern Oscillation. Floods are more likely to occur during La Niña periods. El Niño brings periods of drought.

Australia experienced three La Niña events consecutively starting in 2020. This contributed to the abnormally heavy rainfall and flooding across many parts of the country.

TYPES OF FLOODS

RAIN AND STORMS

After heavy rainfall, rivers can overflow their banks. Even if there is no local rain, a river that has received rainfall further upstream can flood as the excess water moves downstream. Hail that falls during a hailstorm can be very destructive to crops, buildings and cars, as well as blocking drains in streets and causing floods.

One hailstorm in Sydney on 14 April 1999 caused more than $1.7 billion damage.

COASTAL FLOODS

Along the coast, when there is a high tide combined with onshore winds, seawater can flood onto the land. An earthquake on the ocean floor can result in a tsunami that forces a huge wave of water far into the land. These regularly affect Australia's coasts, but they are often quite small. In 1977, a tsunami that was six metres above normal sea level flowed inland at Cape Leveque, Western Australia.

FLASH FLOODS

Flash flooding happens when there is sudden, heavy rainfall that only lasts a short while. Drains in urban areas cannot cope with this unusual amount of water flowing into them, and they overflow onto streets. The force of this water can be extraordinary. It is not unusual for cars and trucks to be swept away.

DESERTS

In the deserts and salt lakes of the interior of Australia, completely dry creeks and lakes will suddenly fill to flood levels during storms, forcing the water across flat deserts that have not been inundated for years. Kati Thanda-Lake Eyre in South Australia periodically fills in this way.

LAKES

Some lakes start to overflow onto dry land even though there has been no rain nearby. This can occur when the lake is fed by underground artesian springs, which have received water from rain hundreds of kilometres away.

DAMS

When water reaches the top of a large storage dam, it will overflow into the waterway beyond. This can cause flooding downstream. To control the effect of this extra water flow, authorities may release flood water from the dam before it overflows, allowing the water to move away before it starts to flood across the land downstream.

LEVEES

A levee is a wall made of concrete, soil or sandbags. Its purpose is to stop flood water from inundating and destroying properties. Levees usually provide only a temporary respite from the flood. They give people time to move themselves, their belongings and their animals to somewhere safer.

FLOODPLAINS

A floodplain is the area of land that might be dry most of the time, except when heavy rainfall causes it to flood. These heavy rainfall events do not happen very often, so people think they will take a chance and build their houses and towns on floodplains.

Land on floodplains is often cheaper than in other locations, making it attractive for people who cannot afford the higher prices. The houses they build are then under threat of inundation when floods occur.

KATI THANDA-LAKE EYRE

Kati Thanda-Lake Eyre is Australia's largest salt lake, measuring 144 kilometres long by 77 kilometres wide. It is 700 kilometres north of Adelaide and is the lowest point in Australia, at about fifteen metres below sea level. It periodically fills with water which then evaporates to leave a salty crust. The amount of water in the lake depends on monsoon rain falling further north and gradually flowing down into the lake.

BIRD MIGRATION

As the lake fills, thousands of waterbirds migrate to it. They include birds that are normally only seen in seaside locations, such as pelicans, gulls and terns. The birds feed on insects and on the small fish that multiply in the lake.

GROWTH EXPLOSION

In summer the lake water evaporates, leaving salt behind. When the lake is full of fresh water, there is an explosion of growth surrounding it. Many of these plants have to grow and produce seeds quickly, before the water dries up.

The plants of Kati Thanda-Lake Eyre attract birds and insects to pollinate them and disperse their seeds. These seeds will then be dormant during the dry months when the lake turns into salt crystals. Migratory birds survive by leaving when the water dries up. Some of them travel all the way back to China and Japan as part of their migration flights.

SAFETY IN FLOODS

The Australian Bureau of Meteorology issues warnings and advice about upcoming floods. They issue different advice depending on the severity of upcoming weather conditions:

FLOOD WATCH ALERT	FLOOD WARNING
Early advice of a developing situation that may lead to flooding.	Advice that flooding is occurring or expected to occur in a particular region.

WATER OVER ROAD

60

The expected flood level will usually be in one of these categories:

1. Minor Flooding
Causes inconvenience rather than major damage.

2. Moderate Flooding
Some houses and main roads will be under water.

3. Major Flooding
Rural and urban areas will be flooded and towns isolated.

PREPARING FOR FLOODS

In Australia, people who live in areas that are prone to flooding are advised to always be prepared and ready to leave to save their lives.

Steps to take to be prepared for a flood:

- Prepare an emergency plan of action that includes what you will take, how you will leave and where you will go.
- Have an emergency kit of necessities always ready.
- Include all the important documents you might need.
- Have contact details for emergency services handy.
- Listen to broadcasts to find out what is happening.

During a flood, there are ways to act that will save lives:

- Never enter flood waters either in person or in a vehicle.
- Follow instructions from emergency authorities.
- Take pets with you.
- Turn off gas, electricity and water supplies to your home.
- Open the door to your fridge so it will not float away and become a danger to others.
- Keep away from fallen power lines.

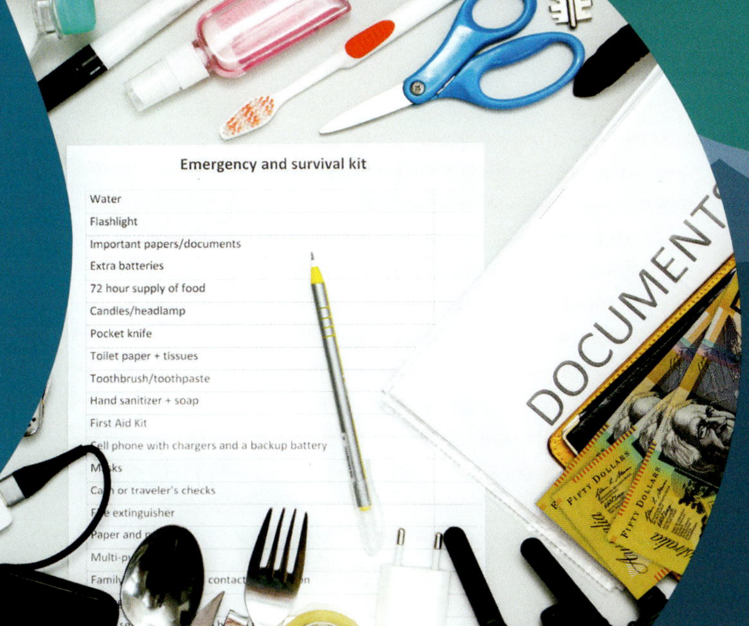

EMERGENCY SERVICES

In Australia, emergency services for people affected by flooding are provided by both volunteers and employees in government organisations.

FIRST RESPONDERS
Organisations that are the first responders to flood emergencies in Australia include:

- **Police**
- **SES**
- **Paramedics**
- **Ambulance officers**

STATE EMERGENCY SERVICES (SES)

These state and territory based organisations are first responders to emergency events such as floods. They assist people and communities facing danger during disasters, and they are a 24/7 service. SES volunteers are recognisable by their uniforms. They undergo extensive training in the use of equipment and emergency vehicles.

SAFETY FIRST

In extreme circumstances, individuals help their neighbours, and small groups of people band together to visit flooded areas and help where they can. While these are praiseworthy and valuable responses, it is important not to get in the way of the professional emergency workers, or to become a casualty yourself.

AFTER THE FLOOD

Once floodwaters fall, the effect of the flood continues. People cannot go back to their normal lives, and sometimes they have to leave an area and never go back.

Houses can be so damaged that they need to be demolished.

Businesses that have been flooded will have all their stock damaged.

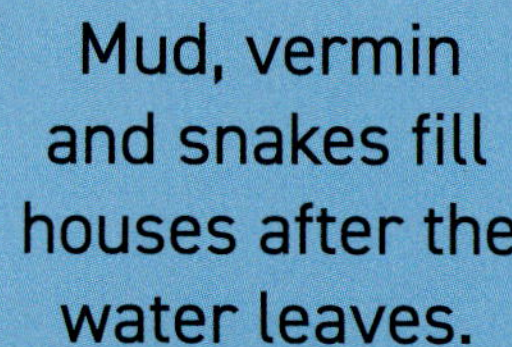

Mud, vermin and snakes fill houses after the water leaves.

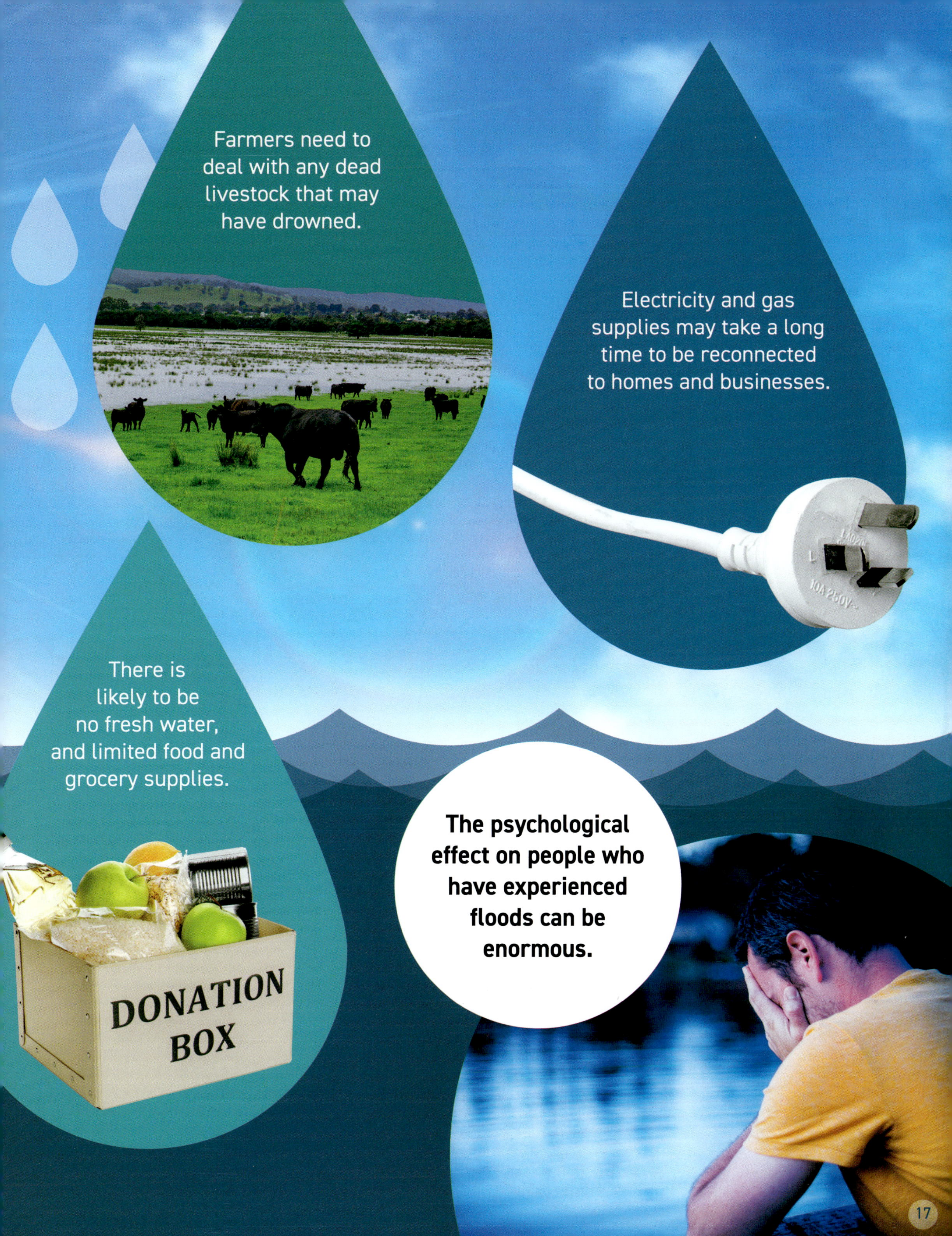
Farmers need to deal with any dead livestock that may have drowned.
Electricity and gas supplies may take a long time to be reconnected to homes and businesses.
There is likely to be no fresh water, and limited food and grocery supplies.
DONATION BOX
The psychological effect on people who have experienced floods can be enormous.

CYCLONES AND FLOODS

The northern part of Australia has a monsoonal climate, like that of Southeast Asia. Annual cyclones are a feature of monsoonal climates, and people living across the Top End know they have to prepare when a cyclone alert is issued by authorities. In northern regions of Australia, most floods occur between November and May because of cyclones. Cyclones were given female names until 1975, when male and female names began to be alternated.

INTENSE WEATHER

Cyclones are intense weather systems, bringing extremely damaging winds and rain. In other parts of the world, this type of weather system is known as a hurricane or a typhoon. Cyclonic wind gusts can exceed 250 kph.

STORM TIDE

A cyclone that is blowing wind onshore will force high waves of seawater to flood the land. Teeming rain will make this situation worse, resulting in extensive flooding. When this type of event coincides with a high tide, this is called a storm tide and the result can be catastrophic flooding.

CYCLONE TRACY

Cyclones that take a path across land do not always result in flooding. If heavy rain continues to fall as the cyclone moves inland, then flooding is likely. In 1974, Cyclone Tracy's destruction of Darwin was mostly a result of high winds.

HISTORY OF FLOODS

Australian Aboriginal people were very familiar with the natural conditions that led to regular flooding of the environment. When the first European settlers started building their towns, the local Aboriginal people noticed that they had chosen a known flood path and tried to warn them, but the settlers ignored the warnings.

As a consequence of ignoring their advice, many settlers lost their lives. They also lost livestock and their towns and farmlands were destroyed. The new towns of Windsor and Liverpool had to be moved to higher ground in the early 1800s, after catastrophic flooding along the Hawkesbury and Georges Rivers in New South Wales.

FLOODPLAINS

The settlers' habit of completely clearing the trees off land beside rivers made flooding much worse than it had been before the 1700s. During heavy rain, the loose soil washed into the rivers, silting them up and forcing floodwater to spread further out onto land, rather than flow downstream and out to the sea.

WORST FLOODS

Damaging, localised flooding is a regular occurrence in most parts of Australia. Some floods are so devastating that their effects are felt far and wide and are remembered for many years afterwards.

To this day the Brisbane river is vulnerable to flooding.

1820s
Brisbane River, QLD

Early European explorers reported evidence of mighty flooding in the areas around the Brisbane River. They found dried river debris high up on trees, and signs that riverbanks had been washed away.

1852
Gundagai, NSW

In 1852, a flooded Murrumbidgee River destroyed the town of Gundagai in New South Wales. Eighty-nine people were killed, which was about one third of the town's population.

Water level marker commemorating the Brisbane flood of 1974.

1955
Maitland, NSW

Between 1954 and 1956, Australia experienced a La Niña-influenced event causing heavy rain to fall over eastern Australia. In February 1955, the Hunter River in New South Wales burst its banks and surged across Maitland in the Hunter Valley. The water spread over an area almost twice the size of Tasmania. Many people lost their lives and photographs and film footage of the devastation shocked Australians everywhere. The damage has been estimated at more than $1.3 billion.

1974
Queensland and the East Coast

Cyclone Wanda hit Brisbane in January 1974, inundating already-saturated land after a wet 1973. More rain later impacted parts of New South Wales and Tasmania. Lives were lost and property was flooded.

1998
Katherine, NT

On 25 January 1998, as a result of tropical Cyclone Les, rain began to fall in Katherine in the Northern Territory, and it continued to fall for two days. The region's average January rainfall was 236 millimetres, but over 900 millimetres of rain fell during that month.

The Katherine, Roper and Daly Rivers overflowed and flooded the town of Katherine. Water in the main street rose to a height of two metres, and more than 1,000 square kilometres of land were flooded. More than 5,000 people were forced to evacuate as floodwaters covered their homes and businesses.

As well as dealing with disease, food shortages and fast-flowing objects, Katherine's rescuers also had to be wary of snakes and crocodiles. Lives were lost and damage was estimated at $70 million.

2010 to 2011
Queensland

Beginning in December 2010 and continuing into 2011, a series of floods devastated parts of Queensland. Flooding was so bad that torrents of water flowed into the Lockyer Valley in what was described as an inland tsunami. Three-quarters of Queensland was declared a disaster zone. Many lost their lives, and over 200,000 people were affected across ninety towns.

Suburbs of Brisbane flooded when the Brisbane River rose to nearly 4.5 metres above its normal level. However, this river level was minimal compared to the eight metres recorded in the Brisbane floods of 1841 and 1893.

2022
Queensland and Northern New South Wales

At the start of 2022, massive rainfall occurred across parts of Queensland and northern New South Wales. This resulted in flood levels that had never been experienced since flood records began in the 1800s. Thousands of homes were flooded, people died and the cost to the economy was counted in billions of dollars. In New South Wales, the Wilsons River at Lismore reached a height of over 14 metres.

2023
Kimberley Region, WA

In the first months of 2023, the Kimberley region of Western Australia experienced the worst flooding ever recorded. Remote Indigenous communities became completely cut off by floodwaters, and ran low on basic food supplies. The Fitzroy River reached a height of 15.8 metres.

CLIMATE CHANGE

Scientists now know that the Earth is experiencing more severe weather events because of human activity. Manufacturing industries and our environmental practices have caused excessive greenhouse gases to enter the Earth's atmosphere. This has led to global warming which has caused our climate to change. The consequences of climate change are far-reaching and include the increasing severity and frequency of floods and storms.

WARMING OCEANS

The temperature of ocean water around the globe is one of the main drivers of cloud formation and rainfall.

As air temperatures rise due to the blanket of increasing carbon dioxide in the atmosphere above us, the extra heat warms the oceans. Warm water releases more moisture into the air, and this contributes to cloud formation and rain events.

WILDLIFE AND FLOODS

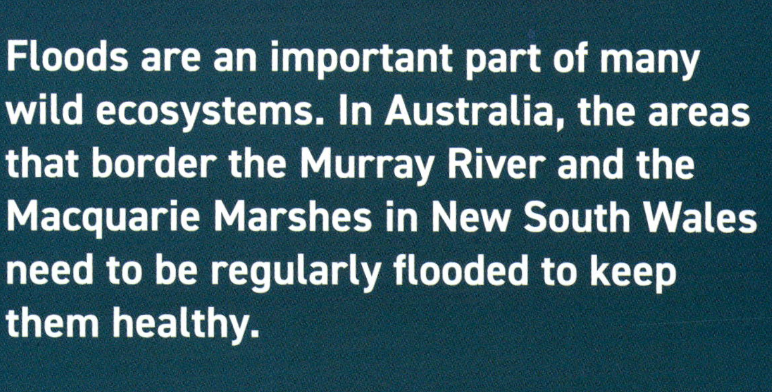

Floods are an important part of many wild ecosystems. In Australia, the areas that border the Murray River and the Macquarie Marshes in New South Wales need to be regularly flooded to keep them healthy.

GRASSLAND AND DESERT

Animals that build burrows in habitats that are normally dry will not have adaptations that let them survive a flood. Burrows of wombats and lizards can become death-traps when flooded. Fast-moving animals such as kangaroos can often get away as flood waters rise, but they may drown if caught in a flooded river. In a flood event, wild animals unused to living in water will suffer from disorientation, cold and exhaustion. This makes them easy prey for feral or lost dogs and cats after a flood.

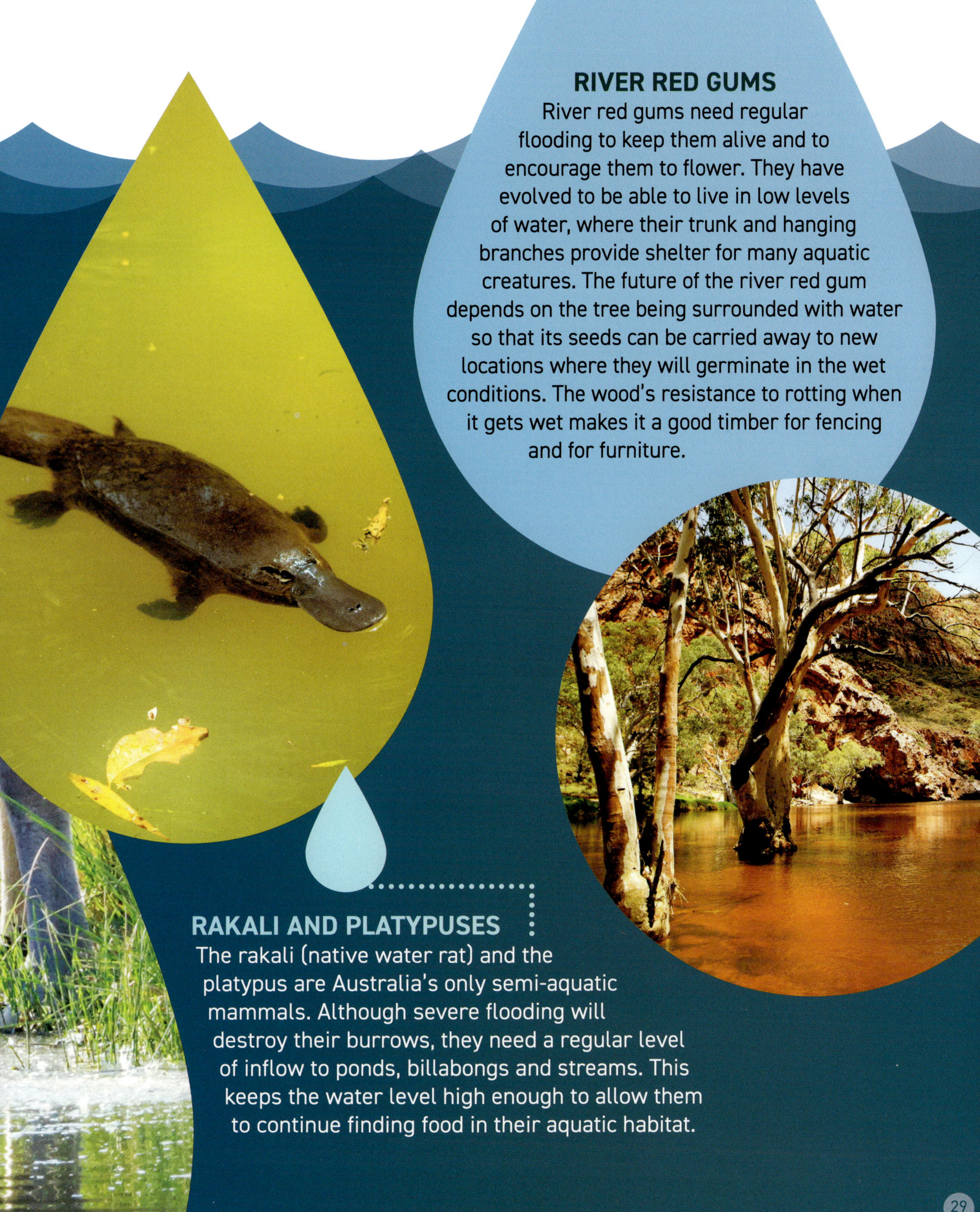

RIVER RED GUMS

River red gums need regular flooding to keep them alive and to encourage them to flower. They have evolved to be able to live in low levels of water, where their trunk and hanging branches provide shelter for many aquatic creatures. The future of the river red gum depends on the tree being surrounded with water so that its seeds can be carried away to new locations where they will germinate in the wet conditions. The wood's resistance to rotting when it gets wet makes it a good timber for fencing and for furniture.

RAKALI AND PLATYPUSES

The rakali (native water rat) and the platypus are Australia's only semi-aquatic mammals. Although severe flooding will destroy their burrows, they need a regular level of inflow to ponds, billabongs and streams. This keeps the water level high enough to allow them to continue finding food in their aquatic habitat.

1 IN 100-YEAR FLOODS

QUESTION

What does it mean when we hear that a flood is a 1 in 100-year event?

ANSWER

This statement means that the height of the flood experienced will probably only occur once in every 100 years. This one occurrence can happen at any time within the 100-year period. This is only a statistic, and high floods can happen at any time if the conditions are right. In recent times, 1 in 100-year floods have occurred far more frequently and are predicted to worsen in severity and frequency. Some scientists are now calling for changes to the flood-mapping system to improve town planning and flood prevention methods.

An artesian bore water cooler in outback Australia cools the water supply

GLOSSARY

AUSTRALIAN FLOODS WORD LIST

alternate repeatedly taking turns

artesian referring to underground water sources

casualty suffering an injury or death

catastrophic life-threatening

debris pieces left behind after a destructive event

dormant sleeping or inactive

inundated completely flooded

levee wall of concrete, soil or sand to stop water flowing onto land

monsoon weather system of heavy rain and strong winds

onshore towards land from the water

periodically happening over regular time periods

pollinate make a plant able to produce seeds

prone to likely to experience

respite period of relief from a problem

tsunami flood of water across land caused by an earthquake

vermin various wild animals, believed to carry dangerous diseases and parasites

Wangi Falls in the Northern Territory are often closed during the wet season due to dangerous conditions.